DESCENT WOMAN

Descent

A Journey for Women

By

Katrina Messenger

Published 2011 Printed by Lulu.com in the United States of America.

ISBN 978-1-257-01195-7

Table of Contents

Preface

Throughout human history, a sacred timeless path has called to women over and over again, the path of descent. And unlike the hero's journey where at each juncture the hero attains gifts, tools, or allies, the descent journey asks us to relinquish our hard won trophies, shatter our deeply held convictions, dissolve our ego-supporting illusions, and surrender our very innocence.

There are many ways a woman can evolve, change and grow over time. In myths, gods descend as well as goddesses; consider Orpheus and Heracles for example. However the number of descending goddesses at all stages of life and standing are remarkable. Inanna, the Queen of Heaven & Earth, answers a call from the underworld, the innocent Kore/Persephone is abducted, matronly Demeter descends into crippling grief, the beautiful Amaterasu withdraws into a cave, and tender Psyche descends on a mission. Even Ereshkigal, the Queen of the Underworld, descends to claim her domain.

And in folklore, the descent motif is also present. Sleeping Beauty falls into a deep sleep, Rapunzel is abducted and placed in a tower, Gretel and Vasalisa are forced to work in the home of the evil witch, and Alice falls down the rabbit hole. And poor Little Red Riding Hood is at the mercy of the wolf on her way to Grandma's house through the deep woods.

My intent is to help women identify, work with and find their place within three timeless descent myths—Kore/Persephone, Inanna's Descent, and what I call Ereshkigal's Ascent.

I use these three myths to develop a Descent Matrix within other myths and folktales. The purpose of this later part is to help women comprehend the many ways these core patterns can express themselves and assist them in uncovering the core pattern within their own life.

Why We Work with Myths

We work with myths because they give us a clear picture into the human soul. Dreams and myth dwell within the same realm, they use the same symbols. That's why I always tell my students: "You want to learn what your dreams mean? Learn mythology." Our psyche pulls mythological themes through our unconscious processes into our dreams. The more you can identify what myth or myths you are living out, the more you can look to the gods for answers. "What did so and so do when faced with this challenge? I wonder if I can contemplate this challenge, in the realm of symbols—in the realm of dreams." So, we study myths because they illustrate the larger patterns of our lives.

Our dreams are highly specific to our personal journey, and myths are like a cultural dream—they represent the journey of a people. There are thematic patterns that repeat across different cultures, which means that these patterns are specific to us as a species. There are also myths that extend beyond the boundaries surrounding our humanity and reflect far greater patterns. Descent myths in particular are greater than human in their content—they illustrate the patterns of life itself.

The whole concept of coming into your brightest, then into the darkness, and ultimately returning to the light is an apt metaphor for the agricultural cycle. It is a way of explaining growth and renewal using the realm of the gods. If you understand how our psychology works, you know that what we see in the world around us are often the very things that we need to pay attention to within ourselves. Too often we miss the messages.

Myths capture the messages in a form that makes them applicable almost immediately.

Many of the following myths and stories has been 'Disney-fied' by well-meaning people who had difficulty dealing with the naked human emotion and raw human experience. I am Old School in this regard; you need to deal with the actual myth. I believe that you should not tone down or make a myth more comfortable; you deal with the reality of it. Maybe the reason for discomfort is that the myth is trying to tell you something about yourself.

This does not mean you cannot translate a few items into modern language where necessary in order to bring clarity to today's audience. I will from time to time, add in some comments that reflect how we need to dig deeper into the meaning of certain passages because the significance of them can be obscure to modern sensibilities. This often involves using parallels or metaphors to assist in that process. But none of these devices are intended to force the myth or folklore to fit within our current day beliefs or customs.

The Journey

We will begin with what I call the Big Three descent myths, Kore/Persephone, Inanna, and Ereshkigal. In each case, I will retell the myth and explore some of the key aspects. I will then construct what I call a Descent Matrix. After we construct the matrix, I will then explain in deeper terms what the story means as a pattern of growth and evolution for a particular stage of a woman's life.

In the second part of the book we will use the Descent Matrix to explore additional myths and stories. The book ends with a challenge to the reader. You are asked to consider your own story whether you are a woman or man. I challenge the reader to create their own Descent Matrix and determine which of the big three myths represents her (or his) journey to wholeness.

Language

The majority of this book is transcribed from audio recordings from my spiritual intensive, Descent: A Woman's Mystery. So it contains questions from participants and is styled as a conversation or lecture. I decided to leave that tone intact, editing only for grammar and readability.

Sources

At the end of the book, I provide a list of recommended books to continue your study of decent myths and to encourage you on your personal descent journey. It is very important to read the full stories for each of the myths and folktales I briefly describe in this book.

Acknowledgements

First I need to thank all the women who attended Descent: A Woman's Mystery over the years. This book would not be possible without your trust and commitment to the journey. Thank you.

Next I need to thank Adam Holland of the Flying Fingers for his accurate and quick transcription. Thank you for saving me months, if not years, of typing.

I also need to thank my students, my colleagues, and my friends for believing in me.

I am grateful as well to my mentor, Dr. Michael Conforti, of the Assisi Institute, for helping me to see myself as if for the first time. You are my Enki, helping me when I most needed it.

Thanks to Rose Miller and Angela Roberts Reeder for editing and proofreading.

And finally I thank lulu.com for making this process effortless.

The Big Three

Descent Patterns

KATRINA MESSENGER

Kore & Persephone

From Maiden to Queen

KATRINA MESSENGER

The Story

There is a beautiful young goddess, Kore, who is out playing in the fields and dancing through the meadows with the other young maiden goddesses. Just having fun, picking flowers, and dancing together. And suddenly, out of the ground grows this incredibly beautiful flower, a Narcissus flower in fact. And little Kore sees this flower and decides, "I must have it."

But as soon as she reaches for the flower, the ground opens up; Hades emerges, abducts her and takes her in to the underworld. And as she's being dragged away she screams, and her mother hears her screams. Now her mother is not just some regular mom; she is Demeter, the goddess of agriculture and civilization. She hears her daughter screaming——and just think, if you are a mother, what that is like, to hear your own daughter screaming. She rushes over but by now the ground has closed back up. "Where is my daughter?"

And the story goes on to describe Demeter's search for her daughter, and her grief because her daughter just simply cannot be found. And she's asking everyone, "Have you seen my daughter? Have you seen my daughter?" And finally Hecate says, "I heard your daughter; she was taken away by Hades."

And so Demeter in her grief—and now rage—demands her daughter back from the child's father, Zeus. But he responds, "You should be happy that I found a good husband for her."

Now, before we continue, we need to stop and comprehend that in many ancient cultures, daughters were handed off to the men their fathers selected all the time. This may seem the most controversial aspect of this myth from our perspective, but in the culture that this myth comes from, this is quite normal.

What is not usual—and why this myth is so powerful—is the mother's rage. And Demeter, in addition to founding the Eleusinian Mysteries in the process of searching for her daughter, also does what I would call the first act of civil disobedience in the history of the world. She says, "If you do not return my daughter, *nothing* will grow. Nothing." Now here is the most important aspect, the ability of a mother to affect the world. "You have to answer to *me*." That is powerful. This is what is controversial about this myth, and this is the part folks often miss.

So in her rage, nothing grows. But guess what? How do the gods get fed? They are fed through our offerings, through our devotion. So what happens when there is nothing with which to feed the gods? Yes, you guessed it. Now all the gods are complaining, "Uh, Zeus? Hello! We're dying here!" And Zeus is like, "Holy crap," and he relents.

In the meantime, you hear very little in the myth about what's going on with Kore. All we know is that suddenly the gods relent and Zeus sends down Hermes to retrieve Kore. But she is no longer Kore.

All this time she had been resisting eating anything in the underworld, knowing that if you eat anything in the underworld, you must stay in the underworld. We can just imagine Hades serving up all her favorite foods arranged along a limitless all-you-can-eat buffet. And Kore is responding, "Oh no, I mustn't!!" But at some point she decides, "I'll just take one little pomegranate seed, that can't possibly be a problem." And with that, she seals her fate. She can leave, but she must also return.

Now here is the other misunderstood part of this story. Folks wonder, "Why on earth did she eat that seed?" It is called the "essential mistake". It is the core of her journey. "You must return to the underworld."

And so imagine, the glorious scene of Demeter's daughter returning, and the joy she must show. That is the agricultural aspect of this myth.

What happens to the ground during winter? The plants appear to die. What happens in spring—a glorious return. Now you can comprehend why this is an agricultural myth. It's not about the rape and abduction of a daughter. It's explaining agriculture and the seasons. She has to go to the underworld, so she can return in the spring.

So now you understand what this myth is really about, and how that understanding of the cycle of the seasons got turned into this powerful story about a mother's rage and a mother's love.

But there is something else here—Kore's transformation into Persephone.

Analysis

So she started out as Kore. And her descent was via abduction. And her underworld was the literal underworld. Her ascent is when Hermes brings her back up.

And would Hermes be a messenger?

Yes, absolutely. The messenger. And when she returns, she is Persephone, the queen of the underworld. And so we complete our first Descent matrix.

Journey	Kore/Persephone
Who is she at the beginning?	Kore
What is descent	Via abduction—Hades
What is her underworld?	The underworld
What is her ascent?	Returned by Hermes
Who is she at the end?	Persephone

What is the mystery that is revealed by Kore's journey? Let us dig deeper into this story.

The Stolen Child

Lord Hades abducts Kore, from her playful romp in the green meadows and descends with her into the underworld. As a youthful goddess, Kore epitomizes the innocence of youth and inexperience—Kore literally means "maiden." Little is shared of Kore's experience within the underworld or her transformation into Persephone, save her ingesting of the pomegranate seeds that requires her to return to the underworld each winter.

Kore/Persephone also represents the seeds of promise, the seeds set aside for planting in the spring, the portion of the harvest set aside to put back into the soil of her mother, Demeter. Kore becomes the Queen of her underworld prison, her incubation gives her power and domain, and her youthful "mistake" assures her annual return to the underworld.

Persephone's return—her ascent—is done in the accompaniment of the messenger god, Hermes. Messengers are one of the few who can enter and leave the underworld at will without repercussions. While they represent the power to communicate, they are also better known for their role as psychopomps, i.e. spiritual guides, mediators across realms, and tricksters.

The Persephone descent is a maiden descent. The woman who needs to work with Persephone usually had their childhood cut short by trauma or betrayal. Her innocence was snatched away as if a part of her died at that critical moment. She often refuses to incubate and as a result, she cannot transform into Persephone and remains Kore or virginal.

The challenge for a Kore is to slow down and come to stillness. She needs to cease romping in the meadow within her memory and bring awareness to her abduction and descent—she must realize where she is and how she came to be there. She needs to call as Kore to Demeter, the mothering goddess within, to fight for her release. She needs to allow this inner parent to literally challenge the gods on her behalf to secure her release. She must accept her hunger and ingest the seeds of darkness and mystery in order to grow into her adult power and ascend into the embrace of womanhood. She must accept the cycles of repose and renewal as the process of continual growth and development.

Her ascent is through the act of mediation between her conscious and unconscious self, between her material and astral self—she must open to her inner maiden and her inner mother.

Inanna, Queen of Heaven & Earth

The Descent of the Queen

The Story

The second story is the story of Inanna. To many, Inanna has become synonymous with descent; however, Inanna has other lessons to teach us. Her descent is only one of her four major myth cycles. These other cycles all occur before her descent, so by the time Inanna descends, she is at full her power. She is already a queen of heaven and earth: she's built her throne, she's retrieved the *Me* (the rules of civilization and the source of her authority), and she has already had her great sex in 'Inanna & Dumuzi'.

So imagine the great Goddess Inanna relaxing and suddenly she hears a call from the great below. Upon hearing this call, she begins preparations for her journey. Immediately we know that this journey is very different from Kore's.

The first thing she does before leaving is to don all her symbols of authority and power. She puts on everything that represents who she is. No one is abducting this goddess. She's at her full power as the queen of heaven and earth.

Next Inanna visits all her temples. These are not temples she built to someone else. There are temples built to her. She visits all the places that are dedicated to her. When she goes to the underworld, she goes under her own power after surveying all within her domain.

Inanna has a servant, Ninshubur. In many myths, the servants of the gods tend actually to be older gods. We can infer that Ninshubur is an older god. Inanna instructs her servant, "Ninshubur, I am going to the underworld. If I am not back in three days, you go get help."

Before we continue with the rest of the story, let us review a couple of the rules of the underworld.

1. If you eat anything in the underworld, you stay in the underworld.
2. Anyone who goes to the underworld is not supposed to return.

So Inanna says, "I hope that I will be back in three days", even given that she is the queen of heaven and earth, "if I am not back, you go get help."

Inanna reaches the first gate of the underworld. Can you imagine, you are a being in the underworld and suddenly you hear a knock? No one goes knocking on the door of the underworld! A lot of people who read this myth do not realize how outrageous this is—you are supposed to *die* to get into the underworld, not stop by for a visit.

Neti, the gatekeeper to the underworld, looks out and thinks, "It's the queen of heaven and earth!" And he goes running down to the queen of the underworld, Ereshkigal, and says, "Inanna is knocking at the gate!"

Ereshkigal slaps her thigh, "She comes to see me? I didn't ask her to come see me. Just lock the gates. Make her come before me naked and bowed." Now think about it, this is Inanna, queen of heaven and earth, and Ereshkigal is saying, "Bring her to me *naked* and *bowed*."

So Neti closes all the gates; goes to the first gate; opens it. As Inanna steps through, he takes one of the symbols of her authority. Inanna complains and Neti answers, "The ways of the underworld cannot be questioned." At every single gate, Neti takes another symbol of her power. Every time she complains and he responds, "The ways of the underworld cannot be questioned."

This is the queen of heaven and earth, and even she knows she cannot violate the rules of the underworld. She knew that before she began her journey and yet she still came. And at every gate, all the things she put on get taken away, until she winds up in front of the queen of the underworld, Ereshkigal, naked and bowed.

Ereshkigal hands Inanna over the judges of the underworld. But these are Ereshkigal's judges, so they declare "Guilty!" "Guilty!" "Guilty!" And Ereshkigal fixes Inanna with the eye of death, and she dies. And they take her corpse and hang it on a hook to rot.

Even in ancient times, the custom was that you buried your dead. Leaving a body unburied was usually a dishonor. The deceased spirit of the person would not be able to rest. So not only did they kill the queen of heaven and earth, they take her corpse and hang it on a hook, like meat. That's pretty rough. And as soon as they hang her on the hook—and we'll talk about this more in the next cycle—Ereshkigal starts having pains.

In the meantime, three days pass and Ninshubur goes to three different gods for help. "My queen Inanna is in the underworld! She must be saved; she has been gone three days!" The gods are like "Dude, it's the underworld. What did she expect? That's what she deserves. She's on her own." No one helps until she gets to Enki, the god of wisdom.

Enki says, "I got it." He scratches some dirt out of his fingernails and fashions these two beings, the kurgarra and galatur. They neither drink nor eat, they neither sleep nor rest, and he sends them to the underworld. And because they have that liminal quality about them, they can get through the gates. They eventually end up in the underworld throne room where Ereshkigal is in great pain.

"Oh! My insides! Oh! My outsides!" Ereshkigal moans in what sounds strikingly similar to birthing pains "Oh, my insides! Oh, my outsides!" So the kurgarra and galatur sit beside her and do what she does—not mimicking her, but mirroring her. "Oh, your insides! Oh, your outsides!"

Ereshkigal has been moaning in pain all this time, and finally someone acknowledges her pain. This touches her heart.

"I'll give you anything that you want." And she has all this stuff brought to the kurgarra and galatur, but they don't want anything. "Oh, but I must give you something!"

Notice they did not immediately ask for Inanna. They waited until she made the offer. "I must give you something, anything!" They respond "Well what about that meat, that corpse that is rotting on the hook?" And Ereshkigal agrees.

And so the kurgarra and galatur feed Inanna the waters and bread of life to revive her. She is coming back to life; she is ascending. But there is another rule of the underworld: you cannot leave the underworld unless someone takes your place. We learn a great deal about the underworld through this myth cycle.

Inanna is awakened from death, but the rules are that someone has to take her place. So the underworld guards accompany Inanna in order to find her replacement. So she comes back up and there's Ninshubur, and the guards say, "Oh, we'll take her." Inanna says, "No! Ninshubur is loyal. Don't take her."

So they travel further and they come across Inanna's son. And he is laying on the ground with his hair all a mess, and his clothes torn, because he had been mourning his mother. And the guards say, "Oh, we'll take him," and she says, "No! He is loyal. He was in mourning for me."

So then they go to the royal city of Uruk, and they see Dumuzi, her husband and lover. Dumuzi is sitting on the throne in all his finery. Inanna is furious and says to the underworld guards, "Him. Take his ass to the underworld."

Dumuzi takes off like a cartoon character and heads for the hills, and the underworld guards chase him. While they are chasing Dumuzi, Inanna has time to finish her transformation and come out of the madness of returning to life. When Dumuzi is caught, Inanna suddenly realizes the impact of her actions. "What have I done? That is my sweet shepherd man."

When she first returns to earth, she was like "Eh, take him." But now she regrets it, "I did not mean to do that." Enter Dumuzi's sister who says, "We will take turns, so you can have some time with him. I'll take a turn and then he'll take a turn in the underworld." And so Dumuzi gets a little break. He still has to go, but he doesn't have to stay forever. And so that's how the myth ends.

Now Inanna is not just the queen of heaven and earth; having gone to the underworld and returned, she is now the queen of heaven, earth, and the underworld.

Analysis

So, who is Inanna, when she starts her descent? She's the queen of heaven and earth. How does she descend? She descends intentionally. It's the call. We know the call, we've heard the call. And any words you wrap around it to try to explain it, that's still not it. It's just "the call." Inanna hears the call. And that to me is poetic, and is also very powerful to recognize. That's what makes it a universal thing.

Well in a way if she was queen of heaven and earth, it's the only thing that's unknown to her.

Yes. But the key is to hold on to all of that, and realize it is very close, but it is even bigger than that. At some point, you have to hear the call. And the call will come to you. And we'll talk more about that, but yes. She is the queen of heaven and earth, so where else can she go? She is the queen of heaven and earth…what is not within her domain? But the core truth is that she didn't question it, she didn't rationalize it, she answered it. And that is the important aspect of this portion of her story.

Enki's helpers revive her. But she came up under her own power after she was revived. And who is she at the end? Queen of heaven, earth, and the underworld.

Journey	Inanna's Descent
Who is she at the beginning?	Queen of Heaven & Earth
What is descent	She answers the call
What is her underworld?	The underworld
What is her ascent?	Revived and returns under her own power
Who is she at the end?	Queen of Heaven, Earth & the Underworld

Let us again dig deeper.

Maturity Is Key

Inanna, unlike Kore, is a mature goddess. Inanna is the queen of heaven and earth. Inanna has earned her queenship and throne; she has acquired the maturity of her marriage bed. She has struggled and matured; she is at the height of her power, when she turns her ear toward the great below. Inanna puts on the vestments of her authority and visits all her sacred shrines before boldly approaching the seven gates to the underworld. She even instructs her loyal servant Ninshubur on what to do if she fails to return.

She is not abducted unaware or unprepared. She chooses to descend into the underworld. At each gate, the gatekeeper forces her to remove an article representing her authority and power; and at each gate she acquiesces.

Meanwhile Ninshubur, after waiting three days as she was instructed, seeks help for her queen. It is Enki, the god of wisdom (and ultimately the source of Inanna's right to rule) who sends two emissaries to bring about her rescue. Enki's emissaries secure Inanna's release by acknowledging and honoring Ereshkigal's pain.

Inanna, awakened by receiving the bread and waters of life, ascends but must seek someone else to replace her in the underworld. She exempts Ninshubur and her children since they grieved her absence. Dumuzi, her husband, however showed no remorse or loyalty. So Inanna sets the underworld guards to take him. Ultimately, Dumuzi and his sister alternate being in the underworld as Inanna forgives him and she evolves into the queen of heaven, earth and the underworld.

A woman who needs to work with her Inanna descent, is mature and fully within her power. She is aware of her strengths and is willing to step fully into her power. She is often middle aged; she is at the height of her game. She is also aware that something is missing, that there is more to life than accomplishment. She may face a life crisis or a crisis of faith, but at some moment, she decides to take stock, to reflect, to check in with her inner self—and thus begins her descent.

At each juncture she reexamines her motives, her goals, her life choices, stripping more and more away until she faces the source of her discomfort and allows it to pull her under. Again, if she can allow herself to become still and allow the rot, she will emerge ready to shed or alter what is no longer working. The key however is her preparation for the journey. She needs to elicit allies like Ninshubur and divine assistance like Enki. If she receives adequate support and spiritual nourishment, she will emerge ready to question everything. She will become even more powerful than she imagined possible.

The challenge for the Inanna woman is her need for a support network and a spiritual container for the work. If she believes that she is falling apart or somehow losing her mind, she will not enter the underworld she will surrender parts of her own soul instead to the gatekeepers.

If she refuses to let go of her preconceived ideas about her goals or path, she will not meet Ereshkigal and enter the womb of transformation. If she does not have sufficient support and nourishment, she will remain in the underworld too long and cease to remember that she is a queen.

But if she can surrender to the journey and face the dark queen, she can emerge ready to shed what no longer serves her and become fully empowered to rule her own heaven, earth, and underworld.

Ereshkigal's Ascent

Challenging the Light

The Story

Ereshkigal's Ascent is a non-traditional descent myth. And in fact, I had real problems when I was first studying descent myths. It felt like there was something missing. I was reading a book—I forget who it was—when the author made an aside during a discussion about Inanna. It was just this little throwaway sentence at the end of one of the chapters:

"There are those who work the myth backwards."

Wait a minute, that's it? That's all you give me, that one little sentence?

But it was that *one little sentence* which sparked an intense curiosity within me. What does it mean to begin in the underworld? What does it mean to kill the beautiful one? These questions haunted me for years, and finally led to figure out the truth about Ereshkigal.

Ereshkigal comes off as the bad guy in Inanna's descent, but we need to know more about Ereshkigal to fully appreciate her—not only in her role in Inanna's descent but as a goddess in her own right.

There are other stories about Ereshkigal. In one of her great stories, Nergal, the god of war, disrespects Ereshkigal's messenger. The gods throw a party, and all the gods attend, except Ereshkigal. This is because Ereshkigal can never leave the underworld. This is another one of those rules of the underworld.

The gods had a big feast, and Ereshkigal's servant Neti goes up to get her portion of the food. When Neti comes in, all the gods stand and bow because they know that he represents Ereshkigal. Think about that for a moment. All the gods bow to Neti because Neti is there to represent Ereshkigal. That's a hint to who she really is. All of gods show her respect.

Of course, this is a story to teach us something, and Nergal, the god of war, doesn't bow. All the other gods are shocked, "Dude, you don't want to mess with Ereshkigal." Nergal has to visit Ereshkigal to make up for his arrogance, but of course he really isn't penitent. There's a whole story of how Nergal gets his lesson. But part of the lesson is that he falls in love with Ereshkigal. Apparently Ereshkigal is so beautiful that Nergal is seduced once he is in the underworld and he becomes her consort. And so that story tells you a little bit about Ereshkigal that's not present in Inanna's story.

There are also hints in the earlier portions of Inanna's story about who Ereshkigal really is. The first myth of Inanna is the Huluppu Tree, which is the tree that she fishes from the Euphrates and plants in her garden. She waters and tends the tree since it eventually will become the source for her throne and marriage bed—which are the subjects of two other stories about the goddess.

One of key questions for me was where did the Huluppu tree come from. The story begins with a shortened version of the Sumerian creation story ending at Ereshkigal, followed by a brief mention of Enki's trip to the underworld and then suddenly there's a tree." And if you read the symbolism in those initial portions, it is pointing to Ereshkigal as the source of Inanna's power. She's the source of the Huluppu tree.

Student: Wasn't the tree infested?

Yes. In the last half of the story, Inanna seeks help from the hero Gilgamesh because her precious tree is infested with three beings—Lilith, the Anzu bird, and a snake.

Lilith represents, along with the Anzu bird and the snake, a portion of Inanna's future life. Lilith was her sexual passion. The Anzu bird was her standing as royalty, and the snake was her trip to the underworld.

The core point is that Ereshkigal is a much older god. I would go as far as to name her as one of the great mother goddesses or a chthonic and dark goddess. Now we have a better idea of who Ereshkigal is.

Think of Ereshkigal as Inanna's initiator. When you work the myth backwards, you take the Inanna cycle and you turn it on its head. What did I say happened to Ereshkigal as soon as Inanna died?

Student: Pain.

Pain. And what did I say that pain was like?

Student: Labor.

Labor. Who was she giving birth to?

Student: Inanna.

That's one interpretation. But think about that for a while. In an Ereshkigal ascent—because that's what this about, this is an ascent—you work the story backwards. So the beautiful other comes to you, and you slay it! Then your transformation begins. Everyone else had a trip down. She's already down. Her journey is back up to the light.

The journey begins with the slaying of the beautiful other. Consider that, for some of us, it feels like we were born into the underworld. If you are a woman of color, if you are a lesbian, if you have disabilities, if you had harsh economic conditions, if you were a victim of infant sexual abuse, it is as if you were born in the underworld. And you cannot do a descent. You have to come up first.

Light bulbs should be going on around this room. And so, this is your myth. Ereshkigal's ascent is your myth.

If your pattern is Kore/Persephone, where innocence is lost not through your own devices, just snatched away—you have to follow Kore's journey. You must surrender to the process and call upon your Demeter to help you. If your pattern is Inanna, then you are in your full power and you must descend willingly.

But if you're dealing with an Ereshkigal ascent, you must slay that beautiful other that is oppressing you, because one of the problems is that you are holding yourself to a standard that is just not real. You are always ugly; you are always a mess in comparison to that image of perfection. So you have to slay that perfectionism. You have to slay your Inanna.

And what happens as soon as you do that? Who do you give birth to? Yourself. You give birth to yourself. And then you take your powers back. "This is mine!" And you come **up** to your authority; you come **up** to your power. Get it? You come up to your full power. That is an Ereshkigal ascent.

Student: So would it be your beautiful self too?

The beautiful other is whatever it is that is holding you down, that you are somehow less because of it. So whatever your beautiful other is, it could be smart, it could be beautiful, it could be healthy, it could be rich, it could be any number of things, but whatever it is, it has to die.

For me personally, because I went through this, I literally had a dream where the beautiful sister showed up, and I killed her.

Analysis

The core issue of an Ereshkigal ascent is to come up from the underworld and take on your power, whereas in an Inanna descent you give up your power. In an Ereshkigal ascent, you take it back.

So, who is she? Queen of the underworld. Her descent? We don't know how she got down there, that's just where she is. You can also be an Ereshkigal ascent if you were a Kore who never transformed. And you just got stuck down there.

Her underworld is the literal underworld. Yes, this will change when we get to the folktales. Her ascent is when she slays Inanna. And who is she at the end? Inanna.

And it's been my experience working with women over time that once you come up from an Ereshkigal's ascent journey you almost immediately go back down in an Inanna descent. You have to finish the full cycle.

But you have to come up before you can go down with power. If you go down without power, it's a Kore descent. You have to have power to do an Inanna descent. So, it's not possible for a woman who's dealing with an Ereshkigal issue to do an Inanna descent, because they have to get power before they can go down. Does that make sense?

When Ereshkigal ascends, she becomes Inanna, queen of heaven and earth. Her journey continues because now she must listen for the call as Inanna and descend.

Student: But who is sitting on the underworld throne?

Ereshkigal. If we try to figure out these journeys in linear time, we will always be confused. The thing about myths is it is always *now*. All of it is always immediate.

Journey	Ereshkigal's Ascent
Who is she at the beginning?	Queen of the Underworld
What is her descent?	Unknown
What is her underworld?	The underworld
What is her ascent?	She slays Inanna
Who is she at the end?	Queen of Heaven & Earth (& the Underworld)

If you take the stories as linear, then we'd have to figure out the order of things. But myths are highly symbolic. They are cultural dreams. So how do we work with these stories?

The two actual stories are Kore/Persephone and Inanna's descent, and within Inanna's descent we find out Ereshkigal's role with Inanna. But there is a simultaneous story in there about the path back up for those who are already in the underworld, and so by pulling out Ereshkigal's story, it's like I'm excavating another story within the same story. So in a sense it's like I took the film, and turned it backwards, so it is a new story. And it gives us a hint at what might be possible for us.

It is important to understand that the structure of our brains and our continual struggle to make sense of our reality shapes our comprehension of time as a linear process, which is not what time really is. When you're dealing with the realm of myth and dream, it is possible to go forwards and backwards.

In some of the classes I teach, we go into a dream, and we slow it down to investigate all around, because it's always so much richer than we first realize. So, remember that we are in the non-linear realm when dealing with myths. It is the same realm as dreams, if that helps.

You can just click it, and it goes the other direction, and it is another whole story. It is similar to the Minor Arcana for those of you who are Tarot enthusiasts. There is a story, an initiatory story from the ace to the ten in every suit. And there is also an initiatory story from the ten to the ace. And it is a different story. Same cards, but two different stories. It is the same process, in the realm of myth.

So let us dig down further into Ereshkigal's tale.

Dwelling In the Darkness

Little is known of how exactly Ereshkigal came to rule the underworld; some say she was sexually assaulted or banished. The Sumerian texts agree only that Ereshkigal is due higher praise than all the upper world gods.

But what is known is that she lives in the underworld, bereft of adequate company, food, and clothing. She is enraged by the appearance of her beautiful "sister" Inanna and calls for Neti the gatekeeper to challenge Inanna at each juncture. She slays Inanna and begins experiencing labor pains almost immediately.

Ereshkigal cannot leave the underworld, so say all the gods, and she suffers as a result. She seems cruel, but it is actually her loneliness, hunger, and pain that cause her to strike out at the beauty that dares to enter her domain.

Women who have spent almost their entire lives within the underworld, either due to childhood trauma or oppressive, violent conditions of their environment are working the myth of Ereshkigal. Maybe they were a Kore who decided to stay or maybe they have been there so long, it has become their home. And like Ereshkigal, they believe that they cannot leave.

But there is path out from the underworld. It is hidden in the story of Inanna's descent. Ereshkigal becomes pregnant after slaying Inanna and begins to moan with pain. Ereshkigal can ascend if she is willing to slay the symbol of the beautiful "other" and allow this beauty to incubate within. She must work the Inanna myth backwards.

A woman facing the Ereshkigal story within her life must shed all that is not working and allow herself to become full with life. She must find validation for her pain and suffering, she must slay the ideal, the perfectionism. She must take back her powers one by one till she emerges as the shining queen. She must reclaim earth and heaven as her domain.

~

So, we have the big three stories, and right now you're maybe thinking "Oh, maybe I'm this, or maybe I'm that," but we've got more to look at, because we can find these myths within so many other stories. There's a reason why I picked these three—they're illustrative of all the descent and ascent motifs that follow. These are some of the oldest stories that we have, especially Inanna.

Other Descent Myths

Demeter's Wanderings

A Mother's Grief

Let's go back to Kore and Persephone, because we talked about Kore's process, but there was a twin process here that I only mentioned briefly — Demeter's journey. Demeter is the goddess of agriculture, goddess of the grain. One of her names is Ceres, which is where we get cereal.

And it is not just the grain; we are so bereft of true understanding of some of the words and what they mean. When we say goddess of the grain, most folks just go, "Eh, grain." We do not grasp the true significance of grain.

In an agricultural society, grain is the essence, the source of life. Can you imagine, you have been foraging, and if you are lucky you are filling in with meat that comes every once and while, and somebody drops some grain on the ground and it grows. This means you do not have to constantly move the tribe; that you can stay where you are for a while. Oh my god!

We can put stuff in the ground and it feeds us! Do you get just how miraculous that is for the wandering tribes to actually stop wandering? Wandering was particularly hard on those who were sick or lame. Normally when the food ran out, the tribe or clan would have to move on. And suddenly they figure out how to grow Food!

That is the significance of the goddess of the grain. You have to really get who Demeter truly is within the pantheon. She is *the* mother. De-meter. *The* mother.

Demeter is the life-giving soil that makes it possible for us to live and prosper. We can ground some of it and make something to eat now, and we can store some for later, incredible!

Do you understand now who Demeter is? She is the ever giving mother who never refuses us, the soil that always opens to us, that always gives back. Unconditional love.

And not only did she give us the grain, she taught us the rules of agriculture. "This is how it is done. You tend the plant, but you feed the soil." These are the rules of agriculture. "You do something now, and you are rewarded later".

33

You know when little children get to the point where they actually learn to wait for gratification? Just think, the concept of long term gratification was introduced to an entire culture. The goddess of grain is truly *the* mother.

So here is this great goddess, the one who gives us life and teaches us how to organize ourselves. She provides the literal rules of civilization.

Now the Sumerians got those rules from Inanna. Who stole them from Enki, but that's another story. Well, she didn't actually steal them, he gave them away because she got him drunk; but that's not the point.

Demeter is the one who gave the Greeks the rules, so that they could live. They're life was completely tied to Demeter. That's what's so hard, when we read these stories, to realize who this goddess really is to her people.

So Demeter is very powerful, and of course being a way powerful mother, one of the ways they showed that in the old days was that she had the most beautiful daughter. What's one of the appellations for Demeter, the full breasted one. (Inanna was also multi-breasted. In some of her statues she has a thousand breasts.) Demeter's full breast also implied maturity and the ability to nurture. She is the mother and her daughter is the maiden. Think about that.

So, this is Demeter, the goddess of grain. And she's out doing what a goddess of grain does: "Here is a rule, grow, another rule, grow, grow less, grow more, grow fast, grow slow;" she's out doing her goddess of grain duties. "Give, open, bless, punish;" if you're a gardener you know what I'm talking about. "Confuse, delight", whatever it is that a goddess of the soil does. And her daughter is taken.

Now I had a younger brother, who was like a son to me, die. And I can tell you that is a huge descent into grief, rage, self-doubt and self-recriminations. Why wasn't I there? What could I have done?

Demeter has her own descent. She goes through her own descent into grief and rage. She winds up at a town well, tearing her hair out and just weeping and weeping and weeping, and the daughters of this great king visit the well, and they see this old woman there – because she is no

34

longer looking like her goddess self, she is just so overwrought. And they go, "Oh, you poor woman. Come, come to our house, we will give you a job." Because that is what you do when you help people, you bring them to your house and you take care of them and give them a job.

"We have a new younger brother and you can come be his nanny, come, come." So they take her home with them. And when she steps into the house – because she's actually huge, her head scrapes the top of the doorway and a bit of her power shows, and folks are like "What was that?" but because she is still grieving it fades away.

They do not know they have invited a goddess into their home, and here they are showing kindness to the great mother. The giver of life is in their home. So she starts taking care of the infant son. In her grief, she thinks, "Maybe I can protect this child. Since I could not protect my own, I will protect this one." So what does she do? She does what a goddess does. "I will put him in the fire, and he will become immortal. He will not die because I am Demeter. I am the goddess of life."

So she tends this child and she is going to make this child immortal. But the mother of the child comes in and "Aiiee! My child is in the fire!"

So Demeter stands up, and everyone bows down, because they realize she is the goddess. And the great king builds a temple in Eleusis in honor of Demeter. And Demeter goes to reside in the temple, but as soon as she sits down the grief comes back. Now she is back into this deep, deep sadness and that is when she decides, "That is it."

"All I ever do is give, give, give to you people!" That should sound familiar to some of you.

So she shuts down everything. "I will not allow growth. I will not give until my daughter is returned." And of course the gods relent, and her daughter is returned.

So she gets her daughter back. And because the people of Eleusis treated her so well, she gives them what is called the Eleusinian Mysteries.

The Eleusinian Mysteries were the rituals that never stopped for over a thousand years. The Eleusinian Mysteries were so important that life itself depended on them. When the people of Greece were at war, when the time came to conduct the Mysteries, they would pause the war, do the Mysteries and then pick up where they left off in the war. There is a story that one year when they failed to stop their battles, the gods descended and conduct the Mysteries themselves — they were that important. And the story of Demeter is key to the Mysteries, because for the most part it is a retracing of Demeter's journey.

So, Demeter has her own descent. So, who is she? She is the goddess of grain, yes, but she is *the mother*. The meter. The measure.

How does she descend?

Grief.

Yes. What is her Underworld? This is why I said that it will not always be the same. Grief was how she descended, but where is her Underworld?

She retreated into her palace, to her temple.

She wandered for a very long time.

We could say, here is wander, here is grief, but also, she retired to her temple. Because she went through those stages until she got to her temple all of them were part of her descent. How does she ascend? Her daughter is returned. And who is she? She's still the mother. But she's Demeter, with her daughter back. She won.

Journey	Demeter
Who is she at the beginning?	The Mother (De – meter)
What is descent	Grief - Wandering
What is her Underworld?	Temple ✹
What is her ascent?	Daughter returned
Who is she at the end?	The Mother with her daughter

Which of the big three stories is most related to this one?

I think Kore.

Kind of, yes, it is sort of Kore, but its actually closer to Ereshkigal. It is closer to Ereshkigal's. It has some Inanna in it, because she's fully powerful, but it was as if all her power was used to be the all-giving mother, she always gave, and then she had to stop.

The ideal of herself, that she always gives, had to die. That is why she is like Ereshkigal. Now we can see how the "Underworld" is not always the literal Underworld.

It wasn't completely within her power either.

She could've gone down there herself.

We have to understand that the Underworld has different say, bio-regions. Whereas in the Sumerian, the great goddess can descend, but in ancient Greece, only Hermes, the psychopomp, can cross those boundaries.

Psyche's Journey

The Search for Love

The next myth we are going to look at is Eros and Psyche. Psyche means soul, and Eros means love. So it is the story of love and soul. Might be an important story to learn, huh?

The short version is that Psyche is so beautiful that all the men are afraid to marry her. She is so beautiful, in fact, that people start worshipping her for her beauty. Which really pisses off Aphrodite, you know, the one they **should** worship.

And Aphrodite says "You know what? You don't get to take over my role." She was going to her temples and there was no food there, and the people were like "Oh, we're worshipping this little girl over there called Psyche."

So Aphrodite is not very happy about the state of affairs. She sends her son, Eros (sometimes called Cupid) – and the thing we really have to get over the way a lot of these gods have been diminished: little naked baby shooting arrows! Give me a break. So She sends Eros to exact her revenge.

Additionally she sends a message through the Oracle at Delphi to the parents. Because the parents have no idea what to do "Oh, our dear daughter, we cannot get her married, people are coming here dropping off fruit baskets. What can we do?" And they go to the oracle, and Aphrodite sends a message: "Sorry, your daughter has to marry death", which pretty much means she has to die. And her parents are upset, but yet they still obey the oracle.

So they take little Psyche, dress her up for her wedding, because she's getting married to death – think about that for a moment – and they take her to this high mountaintop, leave her there, and tell her, "Your husband will be here soon."

Because it is the middle of the freaking wild, and they were leaving her to die! And since they were all worshipping her, all the townsfolk were weeping "Oh, poor Psyche."

And Psyche does this really brave speech in one of the versions: "Don't worry, I should be more worried than you, you get to live, *hello?*" kind of thing. And so they all march off and go get drunk or something.

Anyway Psyche is left there weeping and afraid, while waiting for death to come she fitfully falls asleep. And suddenly this warm wind lifts her up. Meanwhile Eros has had a chance to check out Psyche, and of course he falls madly in love with her. And so, Eros sends this Zephyr wind to lift her and bring her into a hidden valley, and deposit her at the entrance to his palace.

So when Psyche awakens, she finds herself in this incredible paradise, and in front of this beautiful palace. And there is no one else around, everywhere she walks there are unseen hands preparing feasts and showing her such beautiful things. It is like door number one, two, and three are all yours! And these disembodied voices are whispering "This is all for you. This is all for you."

And then at night when she goes to bed, Eros comes to her in the darkness as her husband — because that is how they roll in myths, okay. She has the most wonderful time with Eros, and we will just assume that the drapes are closed. But during the daylight hours she never sees him. Everything is so beautiful but she is completely and utterly alone.

So, she starts speaking to her husband in the darkness, "Is there any way my sisters could visit me? They think I'm dead." He says, "Um, that is not a good idea." But after a while, Eros relents, and a message is sent to her sisters to come to the same hilltop where Psyche was left to die. And they're frightened because they believe Psyche is dead. And then a wind comes, lifts them up, and deposits them into this paradise beyond all beauty in front of a palace.

And the door opens and out comes Psyche, as beautiful as ever. Can you imagine? Because in the meantime her sisters could get married because they were not as beautiful as Psyche. Their husbands were rich but it appeared that Psyche had won the lottery.

"Who is this man?" Psyche struggles to explain, giving each of her sisters different stories. And they realize that Psyche has never seen her husband, and become very concerned.

"He could be a monster. You don't even know what he looks like."

And Psyche's responds, "Wow, yeah, you're right!"

"You need to find out, and you need to probably kill him, he's probably going to eat you after a while."

She gives her sisters lovely gifts as they leave. But now all alone again, she is confused.

"What should I do? I am not supposed to look."

So she comes up with a plan. She places a lamp by the bed, and a knife, and after her husband falls asleep, her plan is to light the lamp, and have the knife just in case he's a monster. She lights the lamp, and lifts it up, and finds that she is married to the god of love – the most beautiful god of love. And in her joy unfortunately a drop of oil burns Eros, and he awakens, sees that she has betrayed him and leaves.

Now Psyche is overwhelmed. She had no idea she was married to a god. And now she calls to him "No, no, come back!" She rushes out into the wild searching for him. She wanders in the wilderness, searching for love, searching for Eros.

In the meantime, Eros returns to his mother, Aphrodite. The truth comes out that he did not actually kill Psyche. Aphrodite is enraged. "Not only did you have people worshipping you, you hurt my son. You broke his heart." So she sends the word out: "Anybody finds Psyche, she's *mine!*"

So while Psyche is searching for Eros, she visits the temples of Hera and Demeter. Psyche undertakes all these services at each temple, and offers her devotion, but the goddesses responded, "Normally, I would be right there for you. But you ticked off Aphrodite." They cannot help her, so finally she reaches Aphrodite's temple.

Aphrodite demands, "You must prove yourself worthy." So Psyche is sent to complete all these tasks. But in every task, she always gets help. What she does not realize is that the help is coming from Eros. The last of the tasks is to go into the Underworld to get a special box from Persephone. And this last time, she is told "Do not open the box! Do not open the box! Do not open the box from Persephone!"

Okay everyone, do not think about elephants!

So what does she do, what is her "mistake"? She opens the box, of course, which is what Aphrodite knew she would do. And inside is a spell of sleep which takes her over. And since Eros has been helping her all along, he removes the sleep and puts it back into the box. And then he goes and pleads to Zeus. "I really love her. You need to fix this for me."

And so Zeus calls a meeting of all the gods in Olympus, so that when Psyche returns to Aphrodite's temple she is taken directly to Mount Olympus. Zeus gives her the nectar of the gods to drink, and she becomes a goddess. So now she can marry Eros, and live happily ever after.

Who is she at the beginning? She's human. Who is she at the end? A goddess. What was her descent?

I think there's a couple.

Very good. What was her Underworld?

The house of Eros?

Her wandering.

Her first descent was to the palace of love. How many of us have had a false palace of love? And what was her ascent?

Aphrodite?

Isn't that interesting? Because normally you would think the Underworld was the tough part, right? Her descent was like "Yeah baby! I have the palace, I have the digs, I have the clothes, and I have the jewelry! Got the hot sex every night." And then it was all taken away . "I don't know where I am. I had a taste of love and now it is gone. "

"And then somebody gives me all this work to do. But that's my way out. That's my way back out." So, which one of the big three best describes her journey?

Because you are right, they are several descents here. We have a Kore, because she was a youngster. She became a queen of Eros's castle. And then, she had to know what Eros looked like. That was the great call from below. She had to know. That's why I said the call is different for everyone.

"I have to know."

And the thing is, guess what? To be a goddess, *you have to know*. So her mistake is exactly what she needed to become a god, but if she did not make that mistake she would have remained in that false palace of love. So her journey is like a Kore and an Inanna back to back.

Journey	Psyche
Who is she at the beginning?	Human
What is descent	Left to die, zephyr wind
What is her Underworld?	The Palace of Love
What is her call	I need to know
What is descent	Wandering in search of Eros
What is her Underworld?	Aphrodite's tasks
What is her ascent?	After being revived by Eros
Who is she at the end?	A Goddess

So it is a couple of descents, one of them is into the palace of love, and then there's another descent once she's there, into knowing. But overall, to get from human to goddess, she has to make that mistake.

What is the first decision she made in this whole story? To look, that is the first thing she did of her own volition. Everything else was decided for her.

"You are so beautiful."
"Oh sorry, you have got to marry death!"
"Oh, here is a big palace! But you cannot see me!"

And she finally says, "I am going to look." It was not a mistake. It was essential for her journey

Folklore & Descent

Into the Woods

Vasalisa & Baba Yaga

A Mother's Love

Okay, so we've done Kore, Inanna, Ereshkigal, Demeter, and Psyche. Next up is Vasalisa. How many of you have heard the story of Vasalisa? This is a Russian tale.

Vasalisa is a little girl, like most tales of this type, whose mother dies while she is young.

What is up with the poor beleaguered stepmothers?

Stepmothers everywhere suffer because of these tales. It's because we don't understand what a stepmother means in the language of the mythic. Maybe we will talk more about that later.

So as Vasalisa's mother is dying she says to her, "I have a gift for you. I have this doll." So Vasalisa gets a doll from her mother as a dying gift. And this doll is really cool because Vasalisa's doll can talk, but only to Vasalisa. And the doll always tells her the truth, and gives her really good advice.

Wouldn't that be really cool to have?

"Should I talk to this guy?"
"No, he is a *dog*."
"Thank you, good to know!"

So, Vasalisa has this gift from her dying mother. Think of it as a gift you can only get from family. We could call it her birthright. Vasalisa's doll is a symbol of her mother's love.

And of course her father, being a father in the realm of folklore, gets remarried. And of course this woman has daughters of her own. You see a theme here? Where else have we heard that?

And of course, they don't like Vasalisa — surprise, surprise. So they treat her like…well, you've heard this story before. Maybe we will talk about Cinderella a little later. Cinderella has a different myth cycle, but it is similar. There are so many stories that start this way.

So, it's really dark out, it's winter. Papa is always away; he is never there to protect his first child, his actual biological child. So of course, they are abusing her.

It is really dark out, and they run around putting out all the flames, all the light. And they turn to Vasalisa, "You have to go into the woods and get us fire!"

So imagine if you were Vasalisa.

"Uh, it's...dark out, number one. It's cold out when it's dark out, because it's winter, number two. And it's dark out, so there are dangerous creatures in the forest. Hello? Number three. And did I mention, it is dark out."

"You have to go get us fire." And they're all sitting around complaining, "We are freezing. You, go get us some fire."

So Vasalisa, with her doll and cloak, trudges out into the forest to get fire. Because she is a good girl after all, she does what she is told.

"Damn it. Stupid old people always sending me into the dark to get fire."

And there are all these details about her journey through the forest. At some point she sees a white rider and suddenly it is daytime. And after a while, a red rider goes by, and it is midday. Finally a black rider goes past, and it is night again. Anyway, that's just another part of the story that I am not going to delve into at the moment.

So she is walking through the forest and she comes upon this house in the middle of the deep woods.

A fence made of human bones surrounds it. Let me say that again ...the fence is made of human bones. The posts are skulls. And the house itself has chicken legs ... and is dancing.

For you and me this is plainly a, "I'd go back if I were you" kind of moment..

It is like we are watching a movie shouting, "Don't go into the house! Turn around! Run, Vasalisa! Run!"

But of course Vasalisa thinks, "Well, maybe this house has fire." So she starts toward the door as it opens, and out steps this really old woman, laughing.

Okay, we have got to do the cackle now, because this is the moment for the cackle.

[Moments of hilarity ensues …]

She is cackling away and soon she spies Vasalisa, "Hey you! Come here! What are you here for?"

"Fire, I am looking for fire."

"Get in here and get to work!"

And so basically, Vasalisa goes to work in the home of…who? Baba Yaga.

This is funny, because we Americans read these stories about Baba Yaga and we think Baba Yaga's really cool. If you talk to the Eastern Europeans and the Russians they would say "Baba Yaga? She is the stuff of nightmares. Baba Yaga is not cool! She's *bad!*" We think everything is sort of cool in some way, but remember that is us; that is not how she is viewed in the homeland of this story. Baba Yaga is scary. Baba Yaga is the epitome of evil.

And so she gives Vasalisa these impossible tasks. Wow that sounds familiar? Hmmm. Sounds like Psyche's tasks from Aphrodite.

But anyway, she gives her these impossible tasks, but Vasalisa's doll gives her advice, gets her help, and tells her the right thing to do. And did I mention one piece of advice that Vasalisa's mother gave her daughter? "Never ask too many questions.

So at some point Baba Yaga says, "Oh, do you have any questions?" And Vasalisa asks a few questions, and Baba Yaga answers them and then asks

"Do you have any other questions?" and Vasalisa says, "No." Baba Yaga thinks, "Hmmm. She's been trained well."

At some point, it's best not to ask. I tell my students all the time, don't ask that question because you might not like the answer.

So to make a long story short, we get to some point where she's preparing food for Baba Yaga; she's cooking and cleaning, good old Gretel role, without the brother locked up to be eaten. And she's doing all this stuff and so finally Baba Yaga starts asking **her** questions.

"Well what did you come into the woods for anyway?"

"I came out to get fire."

"And what did you bring with you?"

"Oh, I just brought the doll that my mother gave me on her deathbed."

"*Your mother's gift!?* You brought your mother's gift into **my** home. *Get out!*"

And Baba Yaga throws Vasalisa out.

And as Vasalisa is leaving she takes a burning coal with her. And she takes the fire and returns home. And we can imagine her stepsisters and stepmother sitting around enjoying themselves.

"Ha, ha, Vasalisa's dead."

The door suddenly opens, and "Heeere's Vasalisa!"

"Got the fire."

Imagine what she looks like — twigs in her hair, all worn out and tired with her clothes a dirty mess.

"I got it!"

And Vasalisa places the burning coal into the fireplace, and overnight the fire lashes out and kills the stepsisters and the stepmother. Extinguishes them. And then of course, because it's a folktale, Vasalisa grows up and marries the king — that was the definition of success for women of that era.

So who is she? She is a daughter. What is her descent? She goes into the woods searching for fire. Where is her Underworld? Baba Yaga's house. And what is her ascent? Being kicked out by Baba Yaga. And who is she? She becomes the lady of her household, and ultimately, as these things always end, she becomes the queen.

But here's the thing: Which of the great three does this story have resemblance to?

Inanna.

Inanna? Are you sure?

Hmmm. Well, she doesn't go in with power.

There's some Kore in there. I mean she doesn't have any control over her father remarrying. There's no simple answer here.

She doesn't really have a choice in going into the woods; she's forced. It's almost like she's abducted, but she's not really.

Yeah. It is a type of abduction. Woods back then were not like woods here, where on the other side there's a mall. For those of you who live in a rural area, what is it like on a winter's night to send a child out into the woods alone? It is an abduction. So it is like a Kore.

And unlike Persephone, where her Underworld period is unremarked, here we know something about what happens to her in the Underworld. She is very obedient; she does what she is told. She works very hard. So this is very much like Kore. And how does she return? Hermes returned Persephone but it was in response to Demeter demands.

She reclaims what he mother gave her.

Yes her mother, her mother's love is what gets her out. This is exactly a Kore story. It's her mother who gets her out of Baba Yaga's domain.

Which is exactly like Kore's journey. When she returns, she has what she needs; she is no longer powerless.

Little Red Riding Hood

Into the Belly of the Beast

Next is Little Red Riding Hood. This is where I finally get to do one where I do not have to tell the story. So who is she, at the beginning? She is a girl, she is a daughter, and she is a child. And before you answer, think about it for a second: what is her descent? And what is her ascent? What is her Underworld?

She goes into the woods.

Yeah, but see, she's made this trip to her grandmother's house many times. What's her descent?

The wolf.

Yes! The wolf. She meets the wolf. "Where are you going, little girl?" And she does not know it, but her whole life has changed. So what is her Underworld?

Belly of the wolf.

Well, it is house of her grandmother. And what is her ascent?

Is it killing the wolf?

But who kills the wolf?

Oh, the woodsman does.

It's the woodsman. So who is she at the end?

Doesn't she marry the woodsman?

Is that the ending to the story you heard?

She married somebody. When she grows older.

Yeah, but it is not actually in the tale. She is rescued. But she is still a child, at the end. She does not actually transform. But who is this story most like? Where were her decisions in this story?

Psyche?

No, we are doing the big three. It is like Kore. It is another Kore. Who is the wolf? Hades. And the woodsman is a version of? Hermes. I am training you to see the big three in all the stories going forward.

So she is still a child at the end, but that is okay. Because her descent began when the wolf took an interest in her, and ended when the woodsman came and killed the wolf. So it was not under her power. That is a Kore/Persephone storyline. But in this case, she is still a child. She is changed, but not in the sense of Kore's change. But it is still a descent story, and it is still a Kore/Persephone pattern. Do you see that? Part of the reason we do this is to give you a way of looking deeply and seeing in the pattern what is behind the story.

She is a child and no place in there does she make a decision?

Yes. It is not going to be exact. But it reflects one of the big three. This is important, because when you start looking at your own life, if you are looking for exact matches, this is going to be a problem. You need to know what are the essential elements. She goes down and comes back not because of her own power. That makes it a Kore/Persephone descent. Got it? Good.

Snow White

The High Cost of Beauty

Now here's one of the problems. The actual story is much darker in Grimm's Fairytales. The problem is that most of us are familiar with the Disney version. So just realize that, and at some point in your life plan to read some of the pre-Christian versions. The Brother's Grimm collected these stories from country folk, and these people were not all Christian. They Christianized the stories. And in the Grimm versions you can get a hint of the actual old stories by reading between the lines.

We can go with either version here. If you know the Grimm version, or the Disney version, they will both work for this one. Okay? Everybody knows a version of this story, right? So who is she, at the start?

She's a girl, a pretty girl.

Sometimes I wonder if I should add Psyche to the list as one of the core myths, but Psyche has a mixture of others.   But you immediately whose story this is, right? But we're going to stay with the big three.

What's her descent? Her evil stepmother, the queen along with her magic mirror, decides that she is just too beautiful, so she plots to kill her. So we already know we are in Psyche's realm, right?

But we have to keep going, so her descent is into the woods, to escape. The man sent to kill her decides to let her escape, similar to Eros. "I am supposed to kill you, but…you need to run. Your stepmother is out to get you." So again, it is a journey into the woods.

What's her Underworld? Use the Disney version.

The home of the seven dwarves.

Yes. And there is this whole transformation; she turns from this girl who had been pampered all her life, into a girl who actually works. She starts taking care of the dwarves. But her trials are not over. The queen discovers she is still alive and goes after her in the guise of an old woman who offers her a poisoned apple, but who comes to her rescue?

Prince Charming.

The prince. Her ascent comes through the kiss of the prince. And who does she become?

The queen.

There you go. All right. Of the big three, which is this? It is still a Kore pattern. And you can see that right? We can hear some Psyche in there too, because her story is partially a Kore/Persephone, with Inanna for the second half.

But we can see that when the story starts off, there is no agency on her part. We get some details of what happens in the Underworld, she learns some things, but she does not come back under her own power. So it is truly a Kore/Persephone pattern.

Handless Maiden

How a Girl Becomes a Queen

And the last one we are going to go through is the Handless Maiden. How many of you are familiar with the Handless Maiden?

The handless maiden is the daughter of the miller. A lot of these old stories are about the miller. You know what the miller is? The miller is technology, and in old times the grinding of the grain was considered high tech.

Growing grain was not an easy task. After all the work of growing and harvesting it, you had to separate out the wheat, and then you had to grind it. So here comes the miller, "I'll grind it for you. For a portion."

So the miller did not toil on the land. The miller did not harvest the wheat. The miller took a cut from your harvest, in exchange for relieving you of a burden.

Nowadays they are called consultants, you do all the work and then they hand it back to you for a fee.

So the reason all these stories are about the millers is because millers were not looked upon very highly. They did not toil, they did not farm, they did not harvest; they just had a horse going around in a circle, or a wheel with water going around in a circle. Think about that for a second, and realize what millers were thought of, and you'll get why millers show up in all these old stories, and why it's always their family who gets screwed over. Think about it. This is one way of getting back at the millers. Got it? Good.

It's very important to put these symbols in context, because we tend to go: "Yeah, the miller, whatever," and then we move on, and we don't even know what it means.

So here is this miller, who apparently has decided, "You know what? I don't really want to work at all." So he's not even at his mill, he's out in the forest, just sort of hanging out. And this fellow comes along – who in the Christianized version is the devil, but we are not going to worry about that – and says hello.

The miller greets him in return. They talk for a bit. Then the man says, "I will give you all the riches you can imagine, all that you desire, in exchange for what stands behind your mill."

The miller who is not too bright because after all he is the miller responds, "That's a good deal."

It is like one of those e-mails. "Hi, I am Mugabi, the son of the prince of Nigeria, I have this check for ten million dollars, I need your help."

"I'll give you everything you desire. All you have to do is give me what stands behind your mill."

And the miller thinks, "The only thing back there is an apple tree. Sure! Whatever!"

And he comes home, and his house has been transformed into this place of luxury, and his wife runs out, she is now wearing jewels and beautiful clothes. And he is amazed, and as he is walking his clothes start changing as well. He had no idea what is the bargain he just made.

He tells his wife, "Oh, this is great! I met this guy, and he said he would give us all this in exchange for what stood behind the mill!"

And his wife suddenly falls silent and her face goes white. "Our daughter is behind the mill."

And now the parents are filled with despair because on one hand, they see what power this being possessed, and on the other, they just promised him their only child. Take that in for a moment. Complete stranger, they just promised their child to him.

So now they cry, "What are we going to do?"

And the daughter, because in these tales the daughter is always so pious, "I will do it for you. It is what is best for you."

You and I know how we would feel about this, right? But the daughter is very pious; this is a folktale, she has to be pious.

So the devil, this guy, does not show up for like a year. And when he finally shows up, the mother and father are crying, and he asks, "Where is she?"

"Out back."

So he goes out back and there's the daughter, standing in a circle of salt.

"Okay, you need to get her out of the salt. And I will be back tomorrow."

So the next day he comes, and there's no circle of salt, but she is dressed all in white.

"You need to not let her bathe. She needs to be dirty. I will be back tomorrow."

So they don't let her bathe. And he shows up, and there she is, she's dressed in horrible clothes, she's dirty, but her tears have washed her hands, and her hands are clean.

"Cut off her hands, so I can take her."

The parents are so frightened of him that they cut off her hands.

But now he says, "I don't want her anymore," and he leaves. "I don't want her anymore. Bye."

So here is this girl with no hands, because her own parents have cut them off.

Let that sink in a moment.

But the daughter says, "It's okay, just bind my arms." So they take her arms, and they bind them up behind her back, because she cannot do anything with them anyway. And she says, "It will be too hard on you if I stay here because all I will do is remind you of what happened today, so I will leave."

Take that in.

"I'll just go off into the woods."

So here is this young girl, in the middle of freaking nowhere, no hands, her arms tied behind her back, and she says, "I'll just go, to make it better for you." And she walks into the woods.

Let's just pause here for a moment and can we all say, "What the hell?"

And there she is, wandering in the woods, helpless, all by herself.

And as she is wandering, she comes across this beautiful orchard at the edge of the woods. The orchard is immaculate, and has these beautiful trees with just the most luscious pears. And the trees bend down to her because she is so beautiful, so helpless. In the Christian version the angels are bending down the branches so she can eat. So here she is, this helpless thing, and the trees are letting her eat their pears.

But where is she? She has wandered into a royal orchard. So what happens if you eat from the king's orchard? You die.

So the orchard keeper comes out and starts counting. "Someone's been eating the royal pears! There are pears missing!" So he stays at the orchard one night, and he sees her come across the little bridge into the orchard, and he watches as the tree limbs bend to allow her to eat a pear. "Oh my, it's a ghost, it's a specter, it is evil!"

So he tells the king, and the king says, "We are going to watch tonight together and I am going to catch this ghost." So they are there at night, and they see this beautiful girl, almost floating across the bridge, going up, and the tree bending.

But the king looks at her, her piousness and her beauty, and he falls deeply in love – because that is how it happens in myths and folktales. He falls deeply in love with her and says, "She will be my queen."

Ever wonder why it is always the bachelor kings that are out running around?

Anyway, he falls deeply in love, and marries her, takes her to his kingdom. And you can imagine the whole scene, because nowhere in the folktale does he say, "Will you marry me?" He just says, "She will be my wife. She will be my queen." So she is.

So then – this should remind you of something – he fashions for her, silver hands. But you cannot do anything with silver hands; you are still at the mercy of everyone around you. But she has servants now, and they take care of her.

So after a time, she gets pregnant. And as it always seems to happen in all these stories, she gets pregnant and the king has to go off somewhere, off to war.

You've heard this in other stories about the messenger, right? The king's mother sends a message: "A beautiful son has been born!" and gives it the messenger, and he goes, and then he gets to that special tree by the river, and he gets really, really sleepy because of that guy. Y'know, the one who got her hands cut off? He's still around. And he goes "Sleeeep." And the messenger falls to sleep. And then he switches the message.

The messenger wakes up, takes the message that he thinks was the original, rides off and the message says: "Your wife has given birth to a monster."

And the king sends back: "I will love this child and my wife, I will love them no matter what." The messenger, on the way back, falls asleep again. "Kill them both," is the message that gets back to the king's mother.

"Oh my god, I'm not killing them!" So what does she do?

She says, "You had better run, girl. You better run."

And so the queen has to take her child with her silver hands. But where does she go? Back into the forest. We are starting to see a theme here. So she heads back into the forest, but now she also has to find a way to protect her child as well as herself.

So in the meantime, while she is escaping into the forest, the king finally gets back and finds out what happened. "That's not what I wrote!" And his mother responds "That's not what I wrote!" And now the poor king starts searching for them; for seven years that he searches. But in the meantime, the queen comes across this cottage in the deep woods. The door opens and there is this old woman. She says, "Oh, I've been waiting for you. Come on in."

So she goes in and this old woman cares for her and her child. So for the seven years that her husband is searching everywhere trying to find her, she gets taken care of in this cottage.

One day she's sitting by the river with her child, and like children do, he wanders off and falls into the river.

She tried calling for help but there was no one around. And all she has are these silver hands. So in an act of pure desperation, she plunges her silver hands into the water.

But guess what happens? Her hands turn back into flesh and she is able to rescue her child. And of course now that she has human hands, the king suddenly comes across the cottage. By this time in his journey, he has almost given up hope of ever finding her again and he is bereft.

But the old woman says, "I have been waiting for you." He enters the cottage and notices a really lovely woman and a young boy. And there is this whole arc where, slowly the truth is revealed to him and there is a grand reunion. And then they all go lie happily ever after. Long story, huh?

Good story.

Good story. So, the handless maiden, who is she at the beginning? Innocent. What is her first descent?

Getting her hands cut off.

Yeah, so it's that whole process of the deal with the devil. Who made that deal with the devil?

Her parents.

Her father. Who does he resemble?

Zeus.

Yes. What is her Underworld? It's her first wandering in the woods, right? So, no hands, then into the woods.

Who rescues her?

The king.

So she is now a queen with silver hands. So she has no power, she has no agency. So she's a queen with silver hands, which is where she starts off in the next cycle. And what is her descent?

Someone's going to kill you; you've got to go.

It's the whole thing with the switched messages, which sends her back into the woods. But where's her Underworld this time?

The cottage with the requisite old woman.

Yes. Who is the agency of her ascent?

Her child?

It's herself, right? She is the one who does it by reaching to save her child. So now who is she?

She's a whole. She's a queen. And she's a mother. She's full.

She was already queen. Who does that remind you of? It is a Kore, followed by an Inanna. You see that? That's pretty cool, am I right?

What are the origins of this story?

Actually one can find a lot of different versions of it in a lot of different places, but it is European.

We have to remember that this is a folktale, so it has its origins in folk magic, folk ways. It comes from people familiar with the deep woods, hard work, and with a healthy disregard for millers.

The other thing is, the bad guy has been Christianized to the devil, but he is really the trickster. He never takes the daughter. The whole purpose of that whole scenario was not to get the daughter; it was to make the miller sacrifice his own child. To his what? To his greed. His frivolous decision put what was most precious to him actually in danger.

But you never hear about him saying, "Nope, changed my mind, take it all back."

True. He never says take it all back.

And what about the daughter? Why did she leave?

Oh, I don't know. Maybe if your parents don't care enough about you to not sell your soul to the devil, then maybe you don't need to go stay with them. So that gives you another way of looking at her deciding, "Oh, I'll just leave."

The point is again is that daughters were often sold off, so that is not actually the big deal here. The big deal here is the daughter, and what she goes through. Not what brought her to that state.

She doesn't have the benefit of a Vasilisa doll but she is taken care of in the darkness, which is sort of the Kore pattern. And silver hands are nice, it is something on your stumps, and your arms are no longer tied behind her back, but they still cannot be used for anything.

It is not till she gets to the cottage that she is truly nurtured for the first time. It also gives you a hint as to what Ereshkigal's role was in Inanna's descent. This old woman is playing the role of Ereshkigal. Maybe there is a time when you need to rot on a hook. Maybe you need to be in that place where you are responsible for nothing, nothing is on your to-do list, where it is like the sleep of death. Maybe that is a good thing sometimes.

When she's in that cottage, she is in the same mythic space as Inanna. And as to her agency, what revives her is the water, the river. Remember what revived Inanna: the waters of life, the bread of life. The water revived her; it brought her hands back to life.

And it was her decision. It looked useless initially; she had no hands. Why did she put her hands in water? It is a pretty powerful story. And you can see the two great myths.

KATRINA MESSENGER

What is Your Story?

What is your Journey?

So each of these storylines has a descent and a return. Even Ereshkigal has the kind of going down and going back up, because she has to kill Inanna as part of this phase here, before she can start that upward track. Remember what I said? Going front wards, going backwards, both are powerful stories. There is a powerful message in it, either way.

So now it is time for your version of this story. You need to decide for yourself what your story is. So take a few moments and take out some paper, and write down:

- Who
- Descent
- Underworld
- Ascent
- Who.

Start thinking about the story of your life. And maybe, like the handless maiden, you might have multiple descents. So think about: what is *your* story?

If you want to, start where you are right now, then later if you have time then go back and look at an earlier part of your life.

We have reviewed several stories in addition to the big three. Look at the big three first, and try to figure out which one closely resembles the journey you are on right now.

Was your journey of your own volition, or did you hear a call? Or, are you already in the Underworld, and don't have an idea about who you are? Do you have an impossible standard you could never meet? It is not just, "Oh, I cannot center." I'm talking about something much deeper than that: a questioning of your self-worth and value. Because the Ereshkigal one is very deep, if you are in an Ereshkigal ascent you have always been in the Underworld, and you will know if that is your story.

For most of us it is either the Kore or the Inanna story. And for some of us, it's both, like the handless maiden. For a few of us it might be all three.

Once you have selected which myth reflects your pattern, read up on it from several sources. Check in with folks you trust and ask them for their thoughts.

Finding Support

If you can, form a support group, maybe even read this book together. Ask each other for help. "Does this sound right to you?" Compare notes and study the myths together.

Often, in my experience, it does not necessarily track with age. An older woman could be in a Kore pattern, while a younger woman is struggling with an Inanna's challenge. So intergenerational gatherings are extremely helpful.

Ritual

In my intensive, we conducted a ritual where all the women descended together and returned together. This can be very powerful — Kore women sitting hand in hand with both Inanna and Ereshkigal women, all in mutual support.

For the ritual, plan to build the Underworld temple together by placing images and sacred items into a space covered with blankets, pillows, tapestries, and other beautiful items. I usually set up some continuingly playing music to create the atmosphere.

Bring chants and songs, bells and drums, food and beverages into the temple. Take your time and let the energy build slowly as someone leads the group in trance into the Underworld and into Hecate's cave. Pray to Ereshkigal and ask her to help you to transform. Spend time together drawing, singing, and dancing. Support each other as you slowly and deliberately return.

Aftercare

Afterwards, do not plan to travel or separate for a while. Try to do it as a sleepover so the group can be available to each other overnight. In the morning, have a delicious meal together.

I often end the working by having all the women lift a wine glass filled with pomegranate juice. We drink in praise of our commitment to the journey and our own transformation.

Plan to get together at some point in the future and share your stories.

This is truly spiritual work that requires community.

Recommended Reading

Addiction to Perfection: The Still Unravished Bride : A Psychological Study (Studies in Jungian Psychology, 12.). Marion Woodman. Inner City Books, 1982 Apr

Archetypal Patterns in Fairy Tales. Marie-Louise Von Franz. Inner City Books, 1997 Oct

Close to the Bone: Life-Threatening Illness As a Soul Journey. Jean Shinoda Bolen. Conari Press, 2007 Mar

The Complete Fairy Tales of the Brothers Grimm All-New Third Edition. Jacob Grimm, Wilhelm Grimm. Bantam, 2003 Jan

Descent to the Goddess (Studies in Jungian Psychology). Sylvia Brinton Perera. Inner City Books, 1981 Apr

Dreaming The Dark Revised (Beacon Paperbacks). Starhawk. Beacon Press, 1989 Jan

The Eleusinian Mysteries & Rites. Dudley Wright. Ibis Press, 2003 Apr

Eleusis: Archetypal Image of Mother and Daughter. Carl Kerenyi; Ralph Manheim;. Princeton University Press, 1991 Aug

Goddesses in Everywoman: A New Psychology of Women. Jean Shinoda Bolen. Harper Perennial, 1985 Apr

Inanna. Diane Wolkstein. Harper Perennial, 1983 Sep

Life's Daughter/Death's Bride. Kathie Carlson. Shambhala, 1997 Sep

The Long Journey Home. Christine Downing. Shambhala, 1994 Jun

The Middle Passage: From Misery to Meaning in Midlife (Studies in Jungian Psychology By Jungian Analysts). James Hollis. Inner City Books, 1993 Apr

Sisters Of The Dark Moon: 13 Rituals of the Dark Goddess. Gail Wood.
   Llewellyn Publications, 2001 Oct

Soul Quest: A Healing Journey for Women of the African Diaspora.
   Denese Shervington. Three Rivers Press, 1996 May

Women Who Run with the Wolves. Clarissa Pinkola Estes Phd.
   Ballantine Books, 1995 Aug

Katrina Messenger

Dark Beauty: Poems at the Heart of the Darkness.
Lulu.com, 2007 Nov

~

Katrina's Joy
www.katrinamessenger.com

Facebook
www.facebook.com/KatrinaMessenger

Reflections Mystery School
www.reflectionsmyst.org

Connect DC (Public Rituals)
www.connectdc.org

Made in the USA
Lexington, KY
13 April 2015